from below we looked up into one bright fissure

no question of backing down now no question of not getting through

Ahsahta Press

Boise, Idaho

The New Series
#86

the spiders   my arms

Jody Gladding

Ahsahta Press, Boise State University, Boise, Idaho 83725-1580
Cover design by Quemadura
    Cover art: Louise Bourgeois, FEMME, 2007.
    Gouache on paper, 14⅝ x 11", 37.1 x 27.9 cm. Photo by Christopher Burke
    © The Easton Foundation, VAGA, New York, NY.
Book design by Janet Holmes
ahsahtapress.org
Copyright © 2018 by Jody Gladding

Library of Congress Cataloging-in-Publication Data

Names: Gladding, Jody, 1955- author.
Title: The spiders my arms / Jody Gladding.
Description: Boise, Idaho : Ahsahta Press, 2018. | Series: The new series ; #86 | Includes bibliographical
    references and index.
Identifiers: LCCN 2018015135| ISBN 9781934103821 (pbk. : alk. paper) | ISBN 1934103829 (pbk. :
    alk. paper)
Classification: LCC PS3557.L2914 S65 2018 | DDC 811/.54—dc23
LC record available at https://lccn.loc.gov/2018015135

Contents

3

Note

For these poems, through-lines in bold offer a way in. Other words con-
stellate around the through-lines, and readers are free to move about
the page as they please. The poem opens into a three-dimensional
space where things can happen simultaneously. And differently with
each reading.

1

the

    hawthorn

        came

         into

  in   flower

            a

      was my   first

               white

                flame

                  turning

                    the

                      alphabet

                  to

                  kindling

because

why

first

womenan

wanted   also   and

ears   fl**are**d   what

from   did   first   woman   hear

her   **good**

the   are

whorls   those

of   temples   ears

her

vulva   **listeners**

lean closer
let me whisper it to you

4

my ski

fox   deer

tracks

line   **is**   **the**is   a**scar**oss   **of**   **inquiry**

hingell   snow

we're trying

ofolding   to ask

into another

where

landscape

tree

line

opens

1

the icebergs

        calving   to reproduce

what I heard   though   **ice**

        caving

      in   we'd tried

like whales   the women   blue

                that

      and   to tend them   *sang*

the **light**   their

          enormity   it's going

      breaking   so

    off   to

          fully   al

blue   enormous

          changed   though

pods

   disappearing

            any

    too small   question of   how can it

                     be

         saving

                 al

                 right

2
the library

of **water**
houses
snow melt
core samples

you can read through
the history
of glaciers
there

are words for weather
all
over
the
floor
in Berlin
when it rains
plastic tubs
like

plinths

catch what
drips through the library
roof
or skull
since the library
was designed
to re-
semble
the human brain

I
forget

most
of what I read
a library in Alexandria

and then a daughter

library

these columns are

what's left
of the
glaciers
pulled from
the shelves
the **ice**
re-
ceding
what can be
re-
collected

the sheer volume
of
each
glacier
how they encased
the earth
how
they are crossed
by the

light

mote

at   the center   of

a beautiful

each   mistake

snowflake

what

makes

the best

of   it

water

them

turn to

something   unimaginable

crystallizing

drifts

down

soft

lands

vapor

asks

without

a

of   sound

dust

unhinging

        the open   sky

    from

                                blue

the

      in-/out-

doors

                nest

                  cavities

                        her

she's

               all **our shelters**

   changing   in**to**   **open**

                     simple   **work**

        hiber-

          nacula

                                blue

                             f/rock

snow

geese

the force

of   this

their   out**flowing** of

words

argument

the wind

against

use

it

carefully

and

we   every

li**s**tened   day

quietly   **also**   **ours**elves

arranging

diminished

cut

through   thin necks

of brocolli starts

I **wo**ke tu*r*ning **m**y head

slowly

do

if **you** **have to** practice

       leave

    I could pack
    your lunch

want me to   every

     fea**the**r

   nest

braid your

fix   hair?

   in

  place waiting
        for their bus

breakfast?

        with

        their

even   there instrument
  if it's all   cases
hairpins and bones

      then

after

   it's

the chicks   a law   **empty**

have

       won't you need

fledged

      your

        music?

onion

                      don't cry

it'**s** only a thi**n** layer

              of white over

                ne**w** green

she'd been

northern junco

out

rustling among dry leaves

in the front

raking

sorting

through seed hulls

her buttons

because it was

what

a nice

spring **day**

required

of

her

species

red dress

for

her

stand

must

what s**the**

take

won't

to

lay

lying

down

of

how

supine

ther

a thing lies

land

in

solution

from

relation to

something else

is

ar　es

shifting

red

15

now I'm the sick
and wounded creature

so that   others keep

my **bitterness**

their distance

does

not to

from

I think

I'll   **become** to

like

me

my

scars

: cocktail attire

so   ve**r**y   sad

to turn

down

thi**s**   invitation

living   among trees   as I do

the fall   lea**v**es

me
wanting

more
bark   less

plumage

hi there

almost t*hir*ty yea*r*s

walking th*es*e wood*s!*   just now

starting to wave

back

white

yellow sweet

well   *red*

hop   we learned

the summer   **field**

white sweet

clovers   why not

early   *large-leafed*

study   the golden

bog   *rough-stemmed*

tall   rod

why not   *yellow-rumped*

the confusing

common yellowthroat   *yellow*

fall

warblers

wind

another

draft

in   the

fire pit

lifts   ash

that doesn't remember

being

wood

because

fire

is a kind of forgetting

patience   **up**

can have nothing to do

with

waiting

caught

being

that

still

leaf

2

the bell had rung the corridors were filling as we hurried past the one who tends the caskets we paused so i could be introduced this is the one who tends the caskets when the ground's too frozen to bury them the one he tended was coated with dust i knew he'd been looking after it a long time and i felt truly grateful thank you i said i looked him straight in the eye we hurried on though now my husband was sobbing odd i thought since it's not his mother's casket his mother's alive the steps were irregular stone worn smooth i was scrubbing them with matted wool though it wasn't wet enough to clean them i knew this was what i should be doing and the direction i had to go was down cherry trees cut to stumps the other groundskeeper preparing their elegy when we were interrupted by young ruffians playing with matches lost i tried to sketch them a map of the orchards it turned into a map of city streetlights can't we continue asked my colleague looking up from her score

lichen and moss growing from beneath my knee as if i hadn't shaved carefully i tried to pull it out but the
bark loosened all the way down my shin peeling back at my ankle gleamed a cluster of slick pebbles i
couldn't look still it was my limb i'm sure it wasn't grafted there's no scar above the root

on the steps a book of amortization tables for the dead you can borrow that the realtor offered but i use it so i'll need it back amortization why don't they just call it interest rates it's for the dead she said in dry leaves mottled brown fledgling ravens with their parents i lay face down gratified they would come so close their heavy bills their claws at my throat only a little frightening now as in childbirth i want to say i'm fine really to anyone who loves me and would suffer to see me so a letter box inside it a womb the matted furry thing crawling in in that seemed all wrong so I shook it free tore the sac from its nose and mouth asleep in my hand now breathing your eyes they're the strangest color she leaned right across the table to say so i was taken aback having always liked the color of my eyes still i knew what she meant my pupils convex rectangular as a goat's i gazed at her salad through the wire fencing a small fist stuffed clover and grass blades it's wild yet it lets me nuzzle because it knew me as a young bear what luck my tongue along the rim of its mouth a black bear's mouth isn't this black its lips rolled back teeth dangerous as cubs my sister and i laughing whispered far into the night one buck hanging dressed upside down from a tree that was okay but when the hunters got closer all the trees turned to deer i tried elbowing them aside like winter coats on racks the prongs kept tripping me their heads swaying heavy as hems well what was i expecting living where i do the standard treatment for malignancies you had to go in among the stiff enormous wings the birds were being trampled like grapes by attendants in scrubs blood running everywhere you crawled out when your time was up you could go back again in a week i won't i said not that i won't flushing low birds from the trees were they oak partridge no cedar waxwing tips lustrous yellow orange but i'd stayed too long my life had passed in anxious adolescence still a student maybe i could teach i'd yet to amount to anything speckled oversize invasive honeysuckle laden with berries i needed to keep heading north when her cry woke me i knew to take it in though why porcupine quills barbed like fishhooks rose from my

haunches i had birthed and raised my child the winter diet of bark expanding to whimper to howl to moan from below we looked up into one bright fissure no question of backing down now no question of not getting through only how to wedge my body so small the others behind me all gentle creatures urging my legs useless as fish on land but angling my shoulders just so they'd fit another dimension this one can't contain time to go first time to show you i love the way

3

breaking

through

red　　　　　　　　lights

　　　　　　　　　　　　　a siren

earth'

　　　　　　　quickens

surface

　　　　　　　　　　　　　　　emergence

　　　lava　　　　　　red

　　　　　　　　tide　　　　　　　**in-**

wild

fire

to

waking　　　　　a deepened　　　　　　　understanding

emergency

room

full　　　　　of

red

ts

patience

hit

along the me**d**ian strip

lat**e** day

sunlight

through its **e**a**r**

scribe

that

I am

to

the   lightning

writing

not   rive

the   tree

be   contiguous   with   the   river

as

some

d**riven**

thing

rain

branching

1

how

the   **girl**

to

move

light

playing

striking

among

metal

gongs

requires

heavy   *but*

dependent

her

body *ies*

2   with   all   her   force

how   **she**
        to

            check
                                                absorbs

                the

                        gigantic sun
putslls   **it**'s
                    vibration
                                                            called
    close
                                                            damping

            her ribs
                                            against

                    splayed
                                                        the
                                                            gong

                out

43

when

what   words   we   can   read

left

the book

seem   open

too   ad^{un}dressing

in

a

unattainable   sunlit

happiness

room

just

green   this

    maple

wings

twirl   no

   down   wind

                         unsettling

        in   the leaves   phoebe

         noon

        sun   on

                               a

             maple

                twig

surprise

no sudden

   unexpected

                  flitting

tail

good

you're here again

un***d***er the table

n**o**t asking for anythin**g**

but my empty plate

there are
                                                          yellow
                                                 apples   falling
apples   on   branches
                                                                    transparent
          an infinite number
                                                           a grid

          of

          different kinds
                                          where each

horizontal   of
                                     meets
above the   lines   is   happiness

                                     sunlight

the　finest

grasses

will

support

red-wing　　　　　　　　　　　　　　　　nests

whistle

the　mo^{la}st

note　　　　　　　held　　　　wonderful

facets of hoar frost

to the lips

taut　　　　　　　　　by

burdens

till she could walk　　　　　　　　of

I carried　　　　　　ice

her　　　　　　　　bending

the

light

at

my hip

family

         from my father's

          trees   second

library   hung   **sto**ry

         icicles   window

  what   nights   cracked

    it   I   searched   open book

      houses   back   room

         shelves   I've

the   for water   **be**en

    spine   glasses   meaning to

tapped   finish

       just take these

sometimes   he said   half

  leaks   **happen**s   my

       I don't read   **light**fe

         anymore

in praise

of

blandness

                  is this   so familiar as scarcely

experience   to require description

common elder

of

white flower   white pith   **transcendence**

white hair

reconciled with

after losing

his

nature   carte blanche

sense

of

taste

and divested

of

my **faith**er

all those

still preferred

colorful ID's

white

peaches

how

her skirt wafts
   light
    steps
       as
                   years later

                      a birthday present

          she runs

                downstairs

my mother's
   brother gave
    my father
        summer dress   this umbrella
            yellow with
                small **black** **dots**
                  opening
    both wives dead   one spoke   bent now
                  against

                  the

                  rain

a finger

book

in the

mouth

at the time

to stop

the run

when

trusting the stitches

there were still those

to hold

I

lost

places to come back

to

blood

interest

flimsy   **little**

"mender's"   **stalls**

many

were   **remained**   **silently**

     browsing

     standing like horses

left

     sleeping

unshelved

or leaned   against one another   old

a little

in

after

the   books

their   **libraries**

dark

closed

stacks

nervous

I'd **ho**ped to graze quietly

reading this g**ra**s**s**

                                th**e** wind keeps

riffling the pages

she is

one who looks

to   knowingly upon

remnant

an   s**piec**ies

~~art~~istarts

patch   complex

from the

together

selvage   mod**her**n

she   blue

threads   of   sky

through   wet

land

don't   as a

look   old

growth   **joy**ous

back

substitute

as an offering

what

body

doesn't

want

to

turn

questions

back

to ask

to   **the   river**

head

put

words

before you

feed

water

in

dive   its

mouth

the

tongue
language

was first

taught to children

by letting them lick

ho**an**ey

from

each
expressive

letter

carved
a small

into

wooden

organ

pallet

the wind

~~love~~ **is a necessary**

relentless

sound of **myth** the perfect

storm O

there's torn leaves

no twisted

denying **it** free

against **makes things**

our **happen**

skin

the spiders   my arms

what I   mean   full

                                                                   of

                              by   rooted   at the end of the
          have been   laundry   day

                      revising

                                             my
                         is   lines

                                                                          old

          not taproot   stumps cling

              but   with

                              web

                                             all the

                                        entanglements

Acknowledgments

For various lines running through these poems, I'm deeply grateful to my sources: Roland
Barthes, Jen Bervin, Luis Camnitzer, René Char, Bob Dylan, Andy Goldsworthy, Darren Higgins, François
Jullien, Gabriella Klein, Julia Kristeva, Agnes Martin, W.S. Merwin, Michel Pastoureau, Gustaf Sobin, Henry
David Thoreau.

For "red dress," I'm indebted to Louise Bourgeois; for "the library of water," to Roni Horn; for "family," to
Gordon Matta-Clark; for "the icebergs," to Jean Valentine.

Deepest thanks also to the MacDowell Colony for the gift of quiet time.

And thanks to the following journals where these poems appear:
BEST AMERICAN EXPERIMENTAL WRITING [BAX] 2016: "the hawthorn," "the spiders my
    arms," "family,""many silently," "because"
LEAPING CLEAR: "the wind love is," "as an offering," "she is the one who looks"
MAINE REVIEW: "the finest grasses," "the tongue"
ORION: "the spiders my arms," "the hawthorn," "she'd been" (as "scratch")
SPACECRAFTPROJECTS: "girl playing gong," "she puts it out"
TERRAIN.ORG: "my ski," "field study," "breaking through"
WHITEFISH REVIEW: "wind another draft" (as "another draft")

About the Author

JODY GLADDING is a poet and translator with three previous collections of poetry and thirty translations from French. Her awards include MacDowell and Stegner Fellowships, French-American Foundation Translation Prize, Whiting Writers' Award, and Yale Younger Poets Prize. She makes her home in Vermont where her work explores the places that language and landscape converge.

AHSAHTA PRESS

NEW SERIES

AHSAHTA PRESS

SAWTOOTH POETRY PRIZE SERIES

This book is set in Franklin Gothic type
by Ahsahta Press at Boise State University.
Cover design by Quemadura.
Book design by Janet Holmes.

AHSAHTA PRESS
2018

JANET HOLMES, DIRECTOR

MICHAEL GREEN
EMMA HELDMAN
KATHRYN JENSEN
BRITTANY O'MEARA
TESSY WARD